WORLD ALMANAC® LIBRARY OF THE MIDDLE AGES

monks and Monasteries

IN THE MIDDLE AGES

DALE ANDERSON

WORLD ALMANAC® LIBRARY

Please visit our web site at: www.worldalmanaclibrary.com
For a free color catalog describing World Almanac® Library's list of high-quality books
and multimedia programs, call 1-800-848-2928 (USA) or 1-800-387-3178 (Canada).
World Almanac® Library's fax: (414) 332-3567.

Library of Congress Cataloging-in-Publication Data

Anderson, Dale, 1953–
    Monks and monasteries in the Middle Ages / by Dale Anderson.
        p. cm. — (World Almanac Library of the Middle Ages)
    Includes bibliographical references and index.
    ISBN 0-8368-5897-2 (lib. bdg.)
    ISBN 0-8368-5906-5 (softcover)
    1. Monasticism and religious orders—Juvenile literature. 2. Monks—Juvenile literature.
3. Monasteries—Juvenile literature. 4. Church history—Middle Ages, 600–1500—Juvenile literature.
I. Title. II. Series.
    BX2432.3.A43   2005
    271'.009'02—dc22   2005043262

First published in 2006 by
World Almanac® Library
A Member of the WRC Media Family of Companies
330 West Olive Street, Suite 100
Milwaukee, WI 53212 USA

Produced by White-Thomson Publishing Ltd.
Editor: Walter Kossmann
Volume editor: Catherine Burch
Designer: Malcolm Walker
Photo researcher: Amy Sparks
World Almanac® Library editorial direction: Valerie J. Weber
World Almanac® Library editor: Jenette Donovan Guntly
World Almanac® Library art direction: Tammy West
World Almanac® Library graphic design: Kami Koenig
World Almanac® Library production: Jessica Morris and Robert Kraus

Photo credits:
Akg-Images pp. cover, title page, 19, 23, 24, 30, 36 (British Library), 5 (Schuetze/Rodemann), 10 (Jean-Paul
Dumontier), 13 (Jean-Louis Nou), 33 (Amelot), 37 (Tarek Camoisson), 43 (Gerhard Ruf), 31, 34; Art Archive
pp. 8 (St. Benedict Sacro Speco Subiaco, Italy /Dagli Orti), 9 (Galleria degli Uffizi, Florence/Dagli Orti), 11
(Cava dei Tirreni Abbey, Salerno/Dagli Orti), 18 (Dagli Orti); Bridgeman Art Library pp. 4 (Trinity College,
Cambridge), 6, 7 (Galleria dell' Accademia, Florence), 12 (Biblioteca Medicea-Laurenziana, Florence),
16 (Musée Condé, Chantilly, France), 20, 21, 27 (Bibliothèque Municipale, Laon/ Giraudon),
22 (Lauros/Giraudon), 25, 28 (British Library), 35 (Bibliothèque Nationale, Paris), 39 (San Francesco,
Montefalco, Italy), 41 (Kunsthistorisches Museum, Vienna), 42 (Prado, Madrid/Index); CORBIS pp. 14, 15.

Cover: In this illumination, Bernard of Clairvaux (center) leads a group of Cistercian monks.
Title page: In this fifteenth-century illumination, a monk teaches a group of students.

Printed in Canada

1 2 3 4 5 6 7 8 9 09 08 07 06 05

Contents

Words that appear in the glossary are printed in **boldface** type the first time they occur in the text.

Source References on page 45 give bibliographic information on quoted material. See numbers (¹) at the bottom of quotations for their source numbers.

The Middle Ages are the period between ancient and early modern times—the years from about A.D. 500 to 1500. In that time, Europe changed dramatically. The Middle Ages began with the collapse of the **Roman Empire** and with "**barbarian**" tribes invading from the north and east. In the early years of the Middle Ages, western European farmers struggled to survive. This period ended with European merchants eagerly seeking new international markets, European travelers searching for lands and continents unknown to them to explore, European artists creating revolutionary new styles, and European thinkers developing powerful new ideas in religion, government, and philosophy.

What Were the "Middle Ages" Like?

Some people view the period as the "Dark Ages," an era marked by ignorance and brutality. It is true that **medieval** people faced difficult lives marred by hard work, deadly diseases, and dreadful wars, but their lives included more than that.

The Middle Ages were also a time of growing population, developing technology, increasing trade, and fresh ideas. New villages and towns were built; new fields were cleared; and, with the help of new tools like the wheeled iron plow, farms produced more food. **Caravans** brought

silks and spices from faraway lands in Asia. New sports and games, such as soccer, golf, chess, and playing cards, became popular. Musicians, singers, acrobats, and dancers entertained crowds at fairs and festivals. Traveling troupes performed plays that mixed humor with moral messages for anyone who would stop and listen.

Religion, education, and government all changed. Christianity spread throughout Europe and became more powerful. Another major faith—Islam—was born and carried into Europe from the Middle East. New schools and universities trained young men as scholars or for careers in the Church, medicine, and the law. Medieval rulers, judges, and ordinary citizens created **parliaments**, jury trials, and the common law. These changes in the fabric of society still shape our world today.

◄ The English monk Eadwine is shown working on a manuscript in this illustration from about 1170. Monks played an important cultural role in the Middle Ages by copying texts and writing new works on religion and philosophy.

A HISTORIAN'S VIEW

"A hundred years ago the medieval centuries . . . were widely regarded as 'The Dark Ages.' . . . It was an age whose art was barbaric or 'Gothic'—a millennium of darkness—a thousand years without a bath. Today . . . scholarship [has] demonstrated clearly that the medieval period was an epoch of immense vitality and profound creativity."
C. Warren Hollister [1]

▲ A church spire towers over the other buildings of the monastery that sits on the island of Mont-Saint-Michel off the coast of northern France. The monastery was founded here in A.D. 966. The church dates from the eleventh to twelfth centuries.

Historians divide the entire period into two parts. In the early Middle Ages, from about A.D. 500 to 1000, Europe adjusted to the changes caused by the fall of the Roman Empire and the formation of new kingdoms by Germanic peoples. In these years, the Christian Church took form and Europeans withstood new invasions. In the late Middle Ages, from about 1000 to 1500, medieval life and culture matured. This period saw population growth and economic expansion, the rise of towns and universities, the building of great cathedrals and mosques, and the launching of the **Crusades**.

Monks and Monasteries

Religion stood at the center of medieval society. Most Europeans belonged to the Christian Church. Monasteries were an important feature of the Church in the Middle Ages. In these communities, monks and nuns vowed to live according to a set of rules. The word *monk* comes from a Greek word meaning "someone who lives alone." While most monks and nuns did not live alone, they did withdraw from the world.

Monks and nuns were a vital part of medieval society. Their most important task was to pray, and they met several times a day to chant prayers. They believed that by doing so, they helped to ensure the salvation of all society. Monks and nuns had other roles, too. Many monasteries preserved ancient knowledge. Some were important for the high-quality food and other goods that they produced. Finally, some monks and nuns became leaders of the Church in western Europe—the branch of Christianity that came to be called the Roman Catholic Church after the split in 1054 with the Eastern Orthodox Church.

the development of Monasticism

The system of monks living in monasteries is called monasticism. Monasticism was a vital part of the Middle Ages. It began back in the second century A.D., appearing first in North Africa and spreading to the Middle East and western Europe. Important individuals shaped the monastic movement by setting rules for how monasteries and convents should be organized and how monks and nuns should behave.

Origins

Monasteries had many social and cultural functions in the medieval world. At the core, though, they were spiritual institutions—sanctuaries where religious people could dedicate themselves to lives of prayer. The desire to become closer to God by shunning the outside world appeared in Christianity in the second century A.D. Devout Christians, mainly in Egypt, began to isolate themselves from other people by living as **hermits**. These hermits became famous for their great spirituality. They attracted followers who hoped to learn from them.

A pattern emerged. Hermits would live in isolation in caves, but those caves would be in clusters. A church stood in a central location in each cluster, and the hermits walked to it on weekends for services. Some hermits emerged as leaders, and they urged the others to carry out some work to support themselves. Soon hermits were making baskets, ropes, and linens, which were sold in nearby towns.

Not everyone who wanted a more spiritual life could cope with the difficulties of living as a hermit. In the fourth century, some religiously minded people gathered in a community in Egypt.

▼ This fourteenth-century painting of Anthony of Egypt shows him giving his money to the poor before beginning his life as a hermit. He had inherited a considerable fortune at the age of twenty, when his parents died.

Anthony of Egypt

The most famous of the early hermits was Anthony of Egypt, who became a hermit around the year A.D. 270. Abandoning his wealth and position, he first sought the guidance of a holy man. After learning what he could, he tried to live alone in a tomb, but he had already become well known for his spirituality, and crowds gathered around him. Anthony then moved to the desert, where he remained for twenty years. When he felt himself ready to teach others, he left his isolation and gathered a group of followers. A book written about him, called *The Life of Saint Anthony*, helped spread his fame to western Europe.

They lived under a leader named Pachomius, whose directions they promised to obey. They worshiped together and ate meals together.

Moving West

In the fourth century A.D., Basil of Caesarea, a highly educated member of the **clergy**, visited Egypt's holy communities. He decided that Pachomius's community was a better pattern to follow than that of the isolated hermits. Basil decided to establish a monastery in present-day Turkey, and he followed the community pattern, although his monastery was much smaller and more compact than that of Pachomius. Basil stressed the importance of obedience to the leader of the monastery. Monks were required to submit their will to their leader. He also encouraged them to work as well as to pray.

The monastic movement soon spread from the Middle East to Europe. It was introduced first through popular books written about the Egyptian hermits. Soon communities were being set up in western Europe. Based on the eastern models, they marked the beginning of western monasticism. One monastery, L'Abbaye de Lérins, became highly influential. It was founded in about A.D. 410 on an island off the coast of southern France, and it produced learned monks who soon began taking positions as bishops. They helped spread the movement and linked monasteries to the organized Church.

Setting the Rules

In the early sixth century, the work of an Italian named Benedict shaped the future of western

Benedict of Nursia
(A.D. c. 480–c. 550)

Born to a noble family, Benedict was educated in Rome, but he was appalled by the immorality there and left the city to try to live a more spiritual life. He went to live alone in a cave, and he gained fame for his holiness. He was invited to serve as **abbot** of a nearby monastery, but this was not a success—his efforts to guide the monks to a strict life resulted in one of them trying to poison him. Benedict returned to a solitary life, but others gathered around him as followers. Eventually, he founded a monastery at Monte Cassino, high on a hill in central Italy. There he wrote his Rule, which was followed at his monastery and at a nearby convent headed by his twin sister, Scholastica. Benedict died about A.D. 550.

▼ In this painting done centuries after his death, Benedict of Nursia (*right*) hands his Rule to a group of waiting monks. The figure receiving the Rule is probably Maurus, a follower of Benedict who, like his master, was later declared a saint by the Roman Catholic Church.

monasticism. Benedict adopted the spiritual life of a monk, at first living in isolation but eventually starting a community of which he was the leader. Benedict wrote a "rule" for his monks to follow—a document that became known as Benedict's Rule. It was a "how to" guide that explained how monasteries should be organized and how monks should live. Benedict's Rule influenced the monastic movement for centuries to come.

Benedict taught that monks should live a balanced life of prayer and work. He described a daily routine requiring the monks to meet for services at regular times every day. Monks were also urged to work. Benedict was understanding as well. He allowed monks who left the monastery to return if they admitted to their error in leaving, and he rejected the complete physical self-denial of the eastern hermits. He

THE ABBOT'S RESPONSIBILITY

"When anyone takes up the title of abbot, he should govern his disciples by a twofold teaching, that is, let him show all things good and holy by his deeds rather than by his words. . . . Let not one [monk] be loved more than another, unless he finds him to be better than the other in good deeds and in obedience."
The Benedictine Rule (c. A.D. 535) [2]

permitted monks to have warm clothing in cold climates, to have adequate food, and to sleep eight or so hours a night.

Monastic Structure

Perhaps the most important thing Benedict did was to outline the position of the abbot in a monastery. The word *abbot* comes from a Greek word for "father." The abbot was the leader of the monks. Abbots served for life. When one died, the monks themselves chose his successor.

Obedience to the abbot was one of a monk's vows when entering a monastery. The other two vows were stability (to stay in the monastery) and conversion of manners (to change one's way of life to a monastic one). An abbot had to run a monastery according to the Rule and could not exercise his authority any way he wished. Indeed, abbots were supposed to consult with their monks before making a decision (although they did not always do so, and they did not have to act as the monks wished). Abbots were also supposed to act as the monks' teachers and spiritual guides.

Before entering the monastery, monks had to give up all property. They either gave it away to the poor or donated it to the monastery. The monastic community, however, could own lands

◄ Benedict, with hand upraised, shares a meal with his sister Scholastica, who is praying. As the halos around their heads show, Scholastica and Benedict were named as saints by the Roman Catholic Church.

▲ This painting from about 1420 by Fra Angelico shows monks at various tasks around a monastery. The requirement to work was part of a monk's life, although prayer and study were more important. "Idleness is an enemy of the soul," Benedict had written.

and buildings, and noble families gave lands to the monastery when a member entered it. While monks were expected to work, the Rule also allowed people from outside the monastery to carry on the farm work and other tasks needed to sustain the community. The monks were to focus on prayer and study.

The Spread of Monasteries

Benedict's Rule became widely used for several reasons. First, its wisdom and balance made it appealing to monks. Second, powerful people promoted it. Pope Gregory the Great wrote about the life of Benedict in the late sixth century,

praising the monk and his Rule. The kings of the Franks (who ruled what is now France) backed the Rule and helped spread it throughout their lands.

The active support of some leaders for the Rule was vital to its survival. It could have been wiped out in A.D. 577, when the Lombards—a Germanic people who invaded Italy—attacked and destroyed Benedict's monastery at Monte Cassino. The monks were forced to scatter, and Italy was left without any monasteries that followed the Rule. Instead, Pope Gregory's writings and the support of the Frankish kings helped to spread the Rule in other areas.

Other Rules

Benedict's Rule was the most influential monastic rule, but it was not the only one. Indeed, it was not even the first. Evidence shows that Benedict drew on an existing rule when he devised his own. Others who came later wrote rules that were different from his. Groups of monks living in different monasteries but all under the same monastic rule (such as Benedict's) are known as an **order**.

The Irish monk Columbana wrote a rule that called for a much more physically severe life than Benedict's Rule. For instance, Columbana said that each monk should "come weary and as if sleep-walking to his bed, and let him be forced to rise

Cassiodorus and Ancient Learning

The Roman noble Cassiodorus was responsible for beginning one important monastic tradition. Born around A.D. 490, Cassiodorus came from a well-to-do, high-ranking family. He held several important offices in the kingdom of the Ostrogoths, who at the time ruled much of what is now Italy. At around the age of fifty, Cassiodorus decided to retire from public service and to start a monastery in which he would also live. Cassiodorus collected many manuscripts for the monastery's library, not just those by early Christian authors, but also some by **pagan** Romans. He ordered the monks to copy and recopy these works, thus preserving them for later generations. This connection of monasteries with learning continued through-out the Middle Ages.

◀ This church in Saint-Benoit-sur-Loire, in north-central France, is all that remains of a Benedictine monastery built here in the seventh century. Benedict's remains were brought here after his death.

IRISH PUNISHMENT

"He who fails to say grace at table or to answer 'Amen' will be punished with six blows. Also, he who speaks while eating, not because of the needs of another brother, will be punished with six blows."
The Rule of Columbana (c. A.D. 600) [3]

while his sleep is not yet finished." Irish monks were famous for their great discipline. Some spoke prayers while standing in icy water, and others recited their prayers standing with their arms stretched out to form a cross. Irish monks were also honored for their learning, and they

helped spread that learning to mainland Europe while doing **missionary** work of their own.

In what is now France and Spain, the rules of Benedict and Columbana were sometimes combined by monasteries that followed a "mixed rule." In France, as time passed, the harsher rules of Columbana were dropped in many monasteries, which then used Benedict's alone. These monks became known as Benedictines.

Cultural Flowering

In the seventh century, some Irish monks carried their missionary spirit to northern England. They established several monasteries, which became important centers of learning. The monastery on

◀ A pair of Benedictine monks offers a book to a bishop. The monks might have copied the book at the bishop's request, or the book might be offered as a gift. Most monasteries were under the authority of the bishop who oversaw the territory where they were located.

▲ This image was painted in the early eighth century at the twin monasteries in Wearmouth-Jarrow in northeastern England. Jesus sits on a throne in the center, flanked by two angels. The figures in the four corners represent the Gospel writers (*clockwise from the top left*) Matthew, John, Luke, and Mark.

England several times, always bringing books back when he returned north. A lover of learning, he built impressive libraries in both his monasteries. One became home to the English monk and historian named Bede (often called the Venerable Bede), who wrote a history of the Church in England.

ðating time

When did Europeans begin marking a difference between the years B.C. and A.D.? This happened thanks to the English monk the Venerable Bede. His history of the Church in England used the abbreviation A.D. (*anno domini*—"in the year of our Lord") to refer to the dates after the birth of Christ. In fact, Bede did not invent this system; he adopted it from an earlier writer named Dionysius Exiguus. Bede's reputation for learning was so great, however, that his use of the system convinced others to adopt it. The use of the abbreviations B.C., or "before Christ," for the years prior to A.D. 1 did not become common until the eighteenth century.

the island of Lindisfarne in northeastern England became known for its skill in producing illuminated manuscripts, such as the famous Lindisfarne Gospels.

Not all early English monasteries reflected Irish influence, though. One abbot, named Benedict Biscop, returned to his native England from Rome to set up monasteries at Wearmouth and Jarrow. Biscop traveled between Italy and

Monasteries in the East

Monasteries also arose on the eastern shores of the Mediterranean Sea. Each monastic house was able to create its own set of rules. Many, though, based their rules on guidelines laid down by Basil of Caesarea.

Monks in the east often moved from one monastery to another, not showing the same stability as western monks. Eastern monasteries also played a less-active role in education. In the west, some monasteries provided schooling for local children, but that was not the case in the east. Instead, the eastern monasteries were more active in charitable works, and they provided hospitals that cared for the sick, homes for the poor and elderly, and lodgings for travelers.

The Monastery of Saint Catherine was built in Egypt in the 550s by Justinian, one of the emperors of the Byzantine Empire. Justinian built the monastery to house Christians traveling to the **Holy Land** to visit the sacred sites of the Old and New Testaments. It remains a Greek Orthodox monastery.

the need for Reform

In the ninth and tenth centuries, the monastic movement faced two major challenges. First came a basic threat to survival, as armed bands looted monasteries. The other was a deeper challenge, as Church leaders criticized monasteries for straying from Benedictine ideals and tried to reform them.

Difficult Times

Between the eighth and tenth centuries, times were difficult for much of western Europe, and monks in monasteries suffered along with everyone else. From Scandinavia in the north came Viking ships, which attacked the lands that are now England, France, Germany, Poland, and Russia. From the east rode the Magyars—horsemen from Central Asia—who struck at present-day Austria, Germany, and Italy. From the south, Muslim armies crossed the Mediterranean Sea from North Africa to raid and establish bases in southern Europe.

The Viking raids were particularly difficult for monasteries. Being isolated and defenseless, monasteries made tempting targets. More importantly, many held rich ceremonial objects and other valuable goods ripe for stealing. The people living in these defenseless buildings were useful to the Viking raiders, too. The influential leaders could be kidnapped and held for ransom. Monks could be seized and sold into slavery.

In A.D. 793, the monastery on Lindisfarne was one of the first places in England to suffer a Viking attack. Raids continued throughout the years, and many more monasteries were hit. A monastery on Iona, an island off the western coast of Scotland, which was founded by the Irish monk Columbana, was so devastated by a series of raids that the monks abandoned it. In the late ninth century, there was a serious decline in monasticism in England and western France.

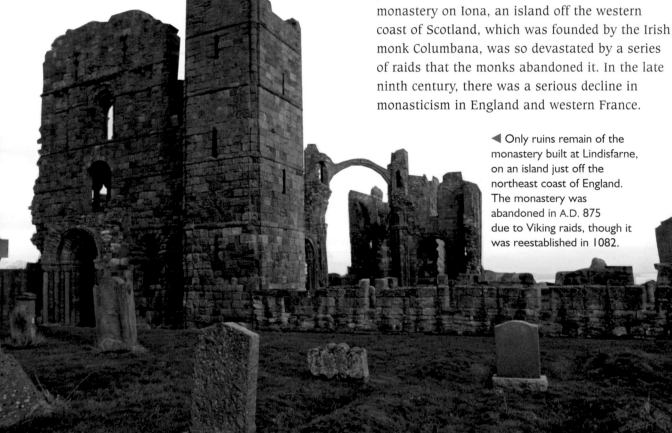

◀ Only ruins remain of the monastery built at Lindisfarne, on an island just off the northeast coast of England. The monastery was abandoned in A.D. 875 due to Viking raids, though it was reestablished in 1082.

Problems Develop

Monasteries were not only physically damaged in Viking attacks, they were also weakened as a result of them. Many monasteries were taken over by nonreligious lords who promised to protect them, but once the lords were in control, the monasteries suffered. Some lords used the money generated by a monastery's lands for themselves. Others placed a relative in charge as the abbot, and sometimes the new abbot went to live at the monastery with his wife. The result was a loss of discipline in many monasteries.

Another problem at this time came as a result of monasteries owning land. As landowners, they were part of the **feudal system** and had responsibilities to the lord who had given them land. Abbots had to provide knights and soldiers to the lord to whom they had given an oath of **fealty**. Abbots were also responsible for operating courts and dispensing justice to the peasants living on their lands. Many abbots were bothered by these roles, which could conflict with their duties as spiritual leaders.

The Cluniac Solution

Laments by Church leaders over the lack of discipline in monasteries led to a push for reform. Leading that reform effort were the monks at a new monastery started at Cluny, in the Burgundy region of what is now eastern France. The Duke

▶ Like other monasteries, the monastery at Cluny had a cloister, which is shown here. The cloister was a covered walkway with arches that surrounded a courtyard or garden. It was attached to the monastery church, and teaching and study took place in the sheltered walkways.

of Burgundy donated the land for this new establishment, but most importantly, he proclaimed that Cluny would be completely independent from him and his heirs. The monastery would be answerable to the pope alone. This step freed the monastery from the kinds of feudal obligations that had bothered abbots.

▼ Odo, the second abbot of Cluny, kneels to receive a blessing from the pope. It was Odo who won the pope's permission for Cluny to set up **daughter houses**, which helped extend the monastery's influence.

THE GRANT TO CLUNY

"May [the monks] have as protectors the Apostles themselves, and for defender the Pontiff of Rome. . . . It has pleased us to set forth in this testament that from this day forward the monks . . . at Cluny shall be wholly freed from our power, from that of our kindred, and from the jurisdiction of royal greatness, and shall never submit to the yoke of any earthly power."
Duke William of Burgundy (A.D. 910) [5]

Cluny's early abbots intended that the monks would follow Benedict's Rule rigorously. Odo, the second abbot, was extremely strict in his instructions. All monks were to be silent except when singing in the monastery's church, although they were allowed to speak psalms as they walked. One monk took this rule so seriously that he allowed a horse to be stolen rather than sound an alarm against the thief.

Growing and Spreading

Odo's fame as a devout monk spread, and soon nobles in nearby areas invited him to take over monasteries on their lands and put his reforms in place. The abbot carried out this work, which spread the influence of Cluny into other parts of France and Italy. Odo was careful to ask for the pope's approval of many of his actions. This tactic helped develop a close relationship between the **papacy** and Cluny.

Cluny became extremely successful. Nobles hoped to gain favor by being linked to its spiritual power, and as a result, they donated lands and other gifts. This not only increased the size of the monastery at Cluny, it also allowed the abbots to set up offshoots of the monastery, known as daughter houses, in other areas. In just a century or so, there were nearly two thousand monasteries in Cluny's religious empire. All the daughter houses, called **priories**, were subject to the authority of the original monastery and its abbot. Most were in France and Spain, but there also were Cluniac priories from Italy to Ireland. Cluny's influence spread in other ways, too. Abbot Hugh was a close advisor to Pope Gregory VII, and another Cluniac, named Odo, became Pope Urban II in 1088.

The original monastery at Cluny grew as well, housing more than three hundred monks in the late eleventh century. At the same time, Abbot Hugh started building a magnificent new church for the monastery. More than 500 feet (150 meters) long and 100 feet (30 m) high, it was the largest church in Europe until Saint Peter's

in Rome was built in the sixteenth century. Even then, it remained the largest church in France.

Reforming the Reformers

With Cluny's growth came added lands, lavish gifts, contact with powerful nobles, and involvement with Church politics. These changes weakened the desire for monastic simplicity. The pressure to expand monasteries led some abbots to lower the standards for admitting people into the monasteries. Many monks showed less dedication to prayer and study. With these changes, Cluny came under increasing criticism. In just a little more than two centuries, the reformers were in need of reform.

Other Reforming Monasteries

Cluny was not the only monastery dedicated to returning to traditional Benedictine practice. Several were set up in Flanders (what is now modern Belgium and France), but more significant than these was the monastery at Gorze in northeastern France. Founded in A.D. 933, Gorze became the center of a large number of related houses, just as Cluny had done. Most were in German-speaking lands. The Gorze monasteries stressed education and provided schooling for local youths.

CRITICIZING CLUNY

"How do they keep the Rule who wear furs, who feed the healthy on meat and meat-fats, who allow three or four dishes daily with their bread, who do not perform the manual labor the Rule commands?"
Bernard of Clairvaux, on the practices of Cluny[6]

The Cistercian Empire

One of the leaders of the new reform movement was a monastery built near the village of Citeaux, just north of Cluny. The monks at Citeaux were called Cistercians, based on the name for this original **abbey**. The Cistercians set strict standards for themselves. They would place their monasteries only on wild, uncultivated lands far from settled areas. They would not accept gifts, such as mills, workers, or baking ovens, all of which might lead to wealth. They would keep their services simple and devote themselves to prayer and work.

Like Cluny, the Cistercians had good leaders. Perhaps the most influential was Bernard. He joined the order soon after it formed and became abbot at Clairvaux, a daughter house. Bernard was a powerful writer and speaker, who spoke out against the abuses of the monks at Cluny and took an active role in Church affairs.

▼ The library at Citeaux, shown here, was built in the fifteenth century, well after the founding of the monastery. Glazed bricks decorate the outside of the structure.

Bernard of Clairvaux
(1090–1153)

Bernard of Clairvaux was one of the most important leaders in the Roman Catholic Church in the twelfth century. Born to a noble family, Bernard received an excellent education. After his mother died in 1107, he decided to follow a more spiritual life. He entered the monastery of Citeaux, where he stayed for three years. In 1115, the abbot of Citeaux gave him the task of starting a daughter house at Clairvaux. Seven relatives and a few other monks joined Bernard in the venture. They suffered many physical hardships until it was well established. These early difficulties worsened Bernard's already poor health; he suffered all his life from many diseases and ailments. As Clairvaux became successful, Bernard became one of the Christian Church's leaders. Some thinkers in the Church tried to use logic and reason to learn about God. Bernard insisted that these attempts were hopeless and that prayer was the proper path for knowing God.

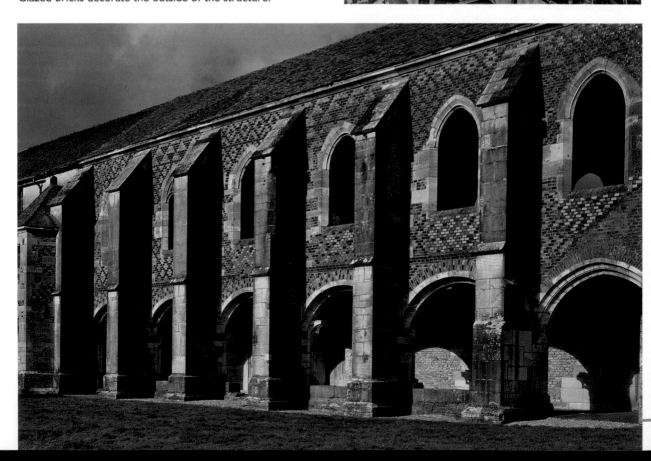

◀ Bernard of Clairvaux (*center*) leads a group of Cistercians. They wear the characteristic white **habits** of the order, which earned the Cistercians the nickname "the White Monks."

The Cistercian order, like Cluny, grew and spread quickly. During the twelfth century, it founded more than five hundred monasteries across Europe. In time all these houses started to accept lay brethren, people who lived in the monastery but did not take the vows of a monk. These lay brethren carried out much of the work needed to support the monasteries. With their efforts, and strong leadership by the abbots, the monastic lands became extremely productive. Monasteries grew wealthy, and the Cistercians, like the Cluniacs, lost their original simplicity.

Carthusians and Canons Regular

Several other reform movements arose as well. A monk named Bruno of Cologne (now Köln, Germany) started a new monastery near the town of Grenoble in southeastern France. The abbey was called Grand Chartreuse, and the monks took the name Carthusians. This was a severe order, totally dedicated to prayer and work. Each monk lived in his **cell**, where he carried out all his activities, including prayer and study. The community only gathered when it was time for church services, for Sunday meals and some other feasts, and for weekly walks. They were to be silent almost all the time.

Other reform groups were the canons regular— groups of ordained priests who lived in a community, like monks, rather than alone. One group of canons regular, known as the Augustinians, were dedicated to serving ordinary people outside the monastery by running schools or hospitals. Another group, the Premonstratensians, also focused on work in the community, though they tended to concentrate on preaching.

the monastic life

uring the one thousand years of the Middle Ages, many different orders of monks developed, each with its own rule, practices, and traditions. It is a mistake, therefore, to think that all medieval monks lived in the same way. Nevertheless, there were similarities and common practices.

Entering the Monastery

People entered a monastery for various reasons. Until the twelfth century, most monks and many nuns entered as child **oblates**. *Oblate* comes from a word meaning "offering"—the children were the parents' gift to a monastery. Parents placed their children in the monastery (for boys) or convent (for girls) to be educated, and eventually these children became monks and nuns.

ENTERING AS A CHILD

"And so, O glorious God, you didst inspire my father Odeleric to renounce me utterly and submit me in all things to thy governance. So, weeping, he gave me, a weeping child, into the care of the monk Reginald, and sent me away into exile for love of thee, and never saw me again."
Orderic Vitalis, *Ecclesiastical History* (1130s) [7]

Most people who entered monasteries came from the noble class. This was true whether they were child oblates or joined voluntarily as adults. According to Benedictine's Rule, monks and nuns had to give up all personal property, and it was important to the monastery or convent that they had property to give. Thus recruits had to come from the groups of people with some land or other property. They did not all come from the upper classes, however. In the sixth century, when Benedict wrote his Rule, he cautioned the abbot not to treat high-born monks better than those from common families. The fact that he gave this advice reveals that there were monks from different

◀ This thirteenth-century painting shows parents offering their son to a monk as an oblate.

Child Oblation

Child oblates tended to come from families that could not otherwise give them an appropriate life. They might be sons who would inherit no land because all the estates were allocated to brothers or daughters for whom no desirable marriage could be arranged. By being placed in a monastery or convent, the child gained the chance to be educated. Boys had a chance to rise to an important position in the Church, which would extend the family's influence. In the twelfth century, Church leaders began discouraging the practice of child oblation, and many monasteries refused to accept children. Eventually, the Church said that only an adult could freely take the vows of a monk or nun. Children could still be placed in a monastery for schooling, and they might choose to take vows, but they could not be promised to the order.

▲ A monk uses a sickle to harvest wheat in this illustration from the twelfth century. The image sits inside a giant Q that begins the Latin word *qui*, meaning "who." Note that the downward stroke of the Q is a sheaf of wheat.

backgrounds. Even peasants could join, as long as they were free and their family had some property to give. One group barred from joining was serfs. These people were not free but were legally bound to the lord on whose land they were born. Since they had no right to leave their lord's land, they could not enter a monastery.

Order in the Order

The abbot was the top official in the monastery. Monks filled other jobs to help with the smooth working of the abbey. The abbot appointed them to these jobs.

The prior was the abbot's second-in-command. He led the monastery when the abbot was away. Some orders put priors in charge of daughter houses. In Benedictine monasteries, deans supervised groups of ten monks each. In Cluniac monasteries, some monks acted as *circatores*, walking around the grounds at different times to make sure that all monks were acting according to the Rule.

Some monks had jobs that were related to the outside world. The cellarer managed the estates, controlled food supplies, and oversaw the labor of those who worked on the farm and at other tasks. The almoner was in charge of the monastery's charitable work, caring for the poor and ill. People in other jobs helped with the running of the monastery: the precentor cared for the monastery's music; the sacristan was in charge of the special clothing and utensils needed in church services and for the altars and chapels in the church; the infirmarian supervised the care of monks who were ill, injured, or aged. The monk who had the special task of training people who were preparing to take their vows was the novice master. The monks-in-training were called novices.

One or two priests lived in the monastery. Their role was to celebrate **Mass** for the monks. They were needed because only **ordained** clergy could lead a Mass, and monks were not ordained clergy. Although the priests were not members of the order, they had to obey the abbot.

A Day in the Life

The central focus of the monks' lives was the series of prayers, called the **Divine Office**, that was said at fixed times each day. Those times were called the canonical hours. In the Middle Ages, there were eight of these times. Matins came at two or three in the morning, when the monastery was still dark. Lauds were said at dawn, when the medieval day began. Prime came at the first hour (6:00 A.M.), followed by terce at the third hour (9:00 A.M.). Sext came at the sixth hour (about noon), and none at the ninth (3:00 P.M.). Vespers were spoken in the evening, and compline, the last, came when darkness fell. Church bells rang out when it was time for each of these prayers. After gathering in the church, the monks sang the prayers that were scheduled for that day. Many of these prayers were from the Book of Psalms in the Bible.

Gregorian Chant

Monks sang a style of music called chant. In chants, a chorus of voices sing without instrumental accompaniment. All members of the chorus sing the same notes at the same time. This music has none of the harmonies of different voices (tenor, baritone, and bass) that are often used in modern music. Several styles of chant existed before Pope Gregory the Great created a standardized form, which was named for him—Gregorian chant. Charlemagne, the king of the Franks, helped spread Gregorian chant by urging Church officials in his kingdom to adopt it.

Later, monasteries began celebrating daily Masses, and other services and practices were added as well. Some monasteries recited the names of saints every day. Others held chapter,

▼ The monks at Mont-Saint-Michel in western France gathered to eat in this room, the refectory. The starkness of the room and the furnishings reveal the simplicity of the monks' lives.

◀ An illustration from a fifteenth-century English manuscript shows monks at prayer. The monks are in the brown habits. The one in front and those on the side have a tonsure—a shaved circle on the top of their heads that marked monks as well as priests.

which was a meeting of all the members of the monastic community. At this meeting, a monk read a chapter of the rule aloud, and the monasteries' leaders discussed any important matters with the members.

When the monks were not praying, they worked and studied. Some worked at copying manuscripts or adding beautiful illuminations to them. Others might pursue crafts, such as metal work or making stained glass. In large and wealthy monasteries, such as Cluny became, monks no longer did manual labor in the fields, as Benedict had required. Hired workers performed these tasks. On the other hand, one of the aims of the Cistercian reform was to return monks to physical labor.

Days were divided according to season. In the summer, monks worked for seven hours and studied for three. During shorter winter days, they studied more than they worked. When the bells sounded for one of the Divine Offices, the monks had to stop whatever they were doing. Prayer was their chief work.

MONKS AT MANUAL LABOR

"As regards their manual labor, so patiently and placidly . . . in such sweet and holy order, do they perform all things, that . . . they never seem moved or burdened in anything, whatever the labor may be. Whence it is [evident] that [the] Holy Spirit works in them."
William of St. Thierry, describing Clairvaux (c. 1143) [8]

Serving the Society

Medieval thinkers viewed society as having three parts: those who fought (knights), those who worked (farm laborers), and those who prayed (monks). Monks' prayers were thought to play a vital role in the world—they could bring blessings to a king or a crop, and they could prevent drought or bring peace. Nobles who donated land or gifts to the monastery hoped that, in return, they would be pardoned for their sins through the prayers offered by the monks in their name. Monks offered their prayers to help save people's souls so they could get to heaven.

Monasteries served society in other ways as well. Benedict's Rule taught monks to accept guests and give them hospitality. Travelers often stopped at monasteries to spend the night on their journeys. Monasteries also provided schooling. Child oblates, who had been pledged to the order, were taught within the monastery itself. It was prohibited to teach outsiders within the monastery, but some monasteries did provide education for local boys by setting up schools in the town. The monastery hired someone from outside the order to teach the classes, which covered basic Latin, arithmetic, and some religious education.

Monasteries provided jobs. A Benedictine priory in Canterbury, England, owned more than

▼ A monk teaches a group of students. The children are probably oblates, who were educated inside the monastery as part of their training to become monks. Monks hired educated men to teach in the monastery schools set up for children of the town outside the monastery walls.

Feeding the Monks

Monks ate two meals a day during summer, when they rose earlier than in winter. Those meals came around midday and in early evening. In winter, they only had one, which they ate in mid-afternoon. Meals consisted of bread and vegetables. According to the Rule of Benedict, only the sick were allowed to eat meat. Benedict's Rule allowed monks to have a small amount of wine with meals. Meals were needed for the body, and mealtimes were also an occasion for spiritual work—while the monks ate, one member of the community read aloud from the Bible. Except for the reader, all monks had to remain silent during meals. As orders like Cluny grew wealthy, rules about meals were relaxed, and food became more plentiful, varied, and tasty.

half the town's houses, and it employed nearly one hundred servants. In addition, scores of tradespeople, from stonecutters to goldsmiths to attorneys, did regular work for the monks. Monasteries that owned **gristmills**, blacksmith shops, or baking ovens provided the services of those facilities to local peasants. Of course, the peasants had to pay a fee to use them, and that fee (like the rents for housing) went into the monastery's treasury.

Finally, monasteries provided pensions of food, clothing, and housing to some people. Local people could buy the right to this pension by giving the monastery property. The pension lasted until the person's death. Some pensions were ordered by nobles who were patrons of the monastery. These pensions were problematical because the abbey received no funds, after the patron's original donation, to cover the pension's cost.

Preserving and Spreading Knowledge

Monasteries played an important part in preserving knowledge. Sitting in a room called the scriptorium, monks copied texts held in the monastery's library. They copied the books needed for the monasteries' religious services and books needed for the boys being taught in the monastery school. They also copied texts for noble clients or Church officials, who paid the monastery for the service.

Monks did not just copy texts. Some also wrote new ones. Being among the most learned people in society, monks produced many kinds of books. The most numerous of these were commentaries on the Bible, but monks also produced biographies of the saints and chronicles describing the history of the monastery or of a region.

▶ Copying manuscripts required careful work. Here, a monk compares a copied text to the original. Despite this care, errors could creep in—and then be passed on to future generations when the original was lost and the incorrect copy was itself copied.

a nun's life

ome women took on the monastic life and lived in convents. As with monks, this practice originated in Egypt in the third century and spread quickly. We know from the writings of the early Church leader Augustine, who lived in the late fourth to early fifth centuries, that there were convents in North Africa as early as that. While convents were not as numerous as monasteries, they existed throughout the Middle Ages. They showed some similarities and some differences from monasteries.

Monastic Women

Most monastic women came from the noble class. When families placed females in a convent, they needed to provide a **dowry** of some sort; usually only noble families could afford to do so. Many religious women, in fact, came from the high nobility and even from royal families. Families expected their daughters to be in the company of others of the same rank. As a result, some convents might have nuns from less distinguished families, while others held women from only the high nobility.

Many nuns were daughters for whom families could not arrange suitable marriages. Some women entered convents to escape a marriage they did not want. Many nuns, perhaps the majority according to some studies, were married or widowed, however. A noble whose wife was unable to produce a male heir might send her to a convent while he tried to annul the marriage so he could marry again. Some married women fled abusive husbands by entering a convent. Nobles and kings also placed aging aunts and mothers in convents. Women who became nuns as adults sometimes posed problems for the **abbess**. Being set in their ways, they were not always willing to obey the rules, and nuns from noble families did not always want to adopt the strict practices of life in a convent. Throughout the Middle Ages, Church officials wrote complaints urging nuns to follow the rules.

Some women who became nuns no doubt did so out of conviction and not due to family considerations. The Roman Catholic Church did

Complaints About Poor Discipline

Bishops often complained about several kinds of behavior by nuns. They protested that abbesses and nuns were too interested in buying the latest fashions when they should wear their order's habit. Bishops scolded nuns for rushing through the Divine Office or, worse, talking during it. Another common theme was pets. Bishops complained that pet dogs ate the food meant to be given to the poor as alms. The biggest complaint, though, was that nuns left the convent and went out into the world.

not allow women to become priests, hold lay positions such as deacon, or even teach. Women, then, had few avenues for living a spiritual life other than becoming nuns.

Girls could enter a convent of their own will at about age fourteen or fifteen. Many were placed there by their families as oblates at an earlier age. Laws allowed these children to decide not to take the vows of a nun and to leave the convent when they became adults. By this time, however, they had spent many years in the convent and

▶ On the right, a hooded woman takes her vows to become a nun. As with monks, women first became novices and underwent training before they finally took their vows to become nuns.

27

received their education there, so most were unlikely to do so. To take the vows and then decide to leave the convent was considered a sin by the Church. If a woman married after leaving the convent, she was **excommunicated** from the Church.

Convents tended to be smaller than monasteries. According to one study, more than half the English convents in the fourteenth century had fewer than ten nuns. A few convents received large endowments (donations) and were able to grow larger. One in Amesbury, England, held nearly two hundred nuns. One survey of English convents from 1350 to 1500 suggests that there were no more than about thirty-five hundred nuns in all of England at any one time.

The Regular Life

Nuns followed the same daily routine as monks. They prayed, observing the Divine Office, as monks did. Meals were taken at the same time, and nuns, too, followed rules of silence for most of the day.

▲ A group of nuns sits in the stalls of the choir, a section of a church. Some appear to be singing—but not all.

Nuns did some of the same work as monks. Some studied, and nuns were among the most educated women in Europe. Devoted nuns, such as Hildegard of Bingen, wrote religious works of great significance. Hrotsvitha of Gandersheim (Germany) produced several works, including six plays and two epic poems with strong moral messages. Isabella of Lancaster, niece of an English king, represents another type of learned nun. She was the abbess of an English convent and ran it well, but she showed little serious devotion to religious life. She spent much of the time away from the convent, living at the royal court. Her writing was **secular**, not religious.

Nuns also worked copying manuscripts. In some German convents, the copying of texts preserved the writings of **mystics** that would otherwise have been lost.

Some nuns taught. All convents, or nunneries, did not have schools; in England, about two-thirds did. Some of the students were oblates, but the nuns also took students—both girls and boys—as boarders. This was one way nunneries could support themselves, because convents were often poor. The nuns charged expensive fees, which kept the population of students fairly low. Many people simply could not afford the fees. The education these children received was not very advanced. They probably learned to read but may not have learned writing.

Nuns rarely did heavy agricultural work, but in the poorest convents, which could not afford to hire workers, they had to. The same was true of housework, which was typically performed by servants. Nunneries that could afford it hired several workers. One managed the convent's lands. Others did the cooking, baking, brewing, and laundry. Nuns who had to do this work often complained about it. Even noblewomen who became nuns were willing to do needlework, though, which was considered to be an acceptable task for a woman of high status. Some orders dedicated themselves to caring for the sick.

Nuns were typically cloistered—shut off from contact with the outside world. They did not always follow this rule, however, and Church officials often sent messages chiding them for leaving the convent. In 1300, Pope Boniface VIII issued a decree that warned nuns never to leave the convent except in the most extreme of cases. The papal pronouncement was not generally obeyed, however. Nuns in one convent in England showed their defiance. They threw a copy of the pope's order at the head of the bishop who had read it to them.

Nuns also often ignored rules about clothing. Some chose to wear the latest fashions even though they were supposed to dress simply in habits. Church officials often wrote nagging letters to nuns urging them to avoid these vanities. They also complained that nuns spent too little time practicing the Divine Office—especially matins, which came in the middle of the night. Another common criticism was that nuns were too interested in dancing.

hildegard of Bingen
(1098–1179)

Hildegard of Bingen (Germany) was a nun—and a poet, mystic, composer, illustrator, and highly respected person in the Roman Catholic Church. She was born to noble parents who placed her, when she was eight, with an **anchoress,** named Jutta, connected to a Benedictine monastery. She learned to read and write and took the vows of a nun at fourteen. Some twenty years later, she became the head of the community of nuns. From childhood, Hildegard experienced mystical visions. When she was in her forties, a committee of Church officials reviewed her statements about these visions and decided that they were true spiritual insights provided by God and not **heresy**. She wrote many poems and set some to music. She also exchanged letters with many Church leaders, who sought her views on various issues.

► Along with taking part in the Divine Office, nuns often made private prayers. In the upper left corner, this woman is receiving a blessing, perhaps from the abbess. In the other panels, nuns pray to Mary and Jesus (top right) and to two saints.

Changing Status

From the fifth to the ninth centuries, present-day France and England had many double monasteries, with separate facilities for men and women in the same complex. In this period, an abbess—usually the daughter of a high noble or king—led the institution.

However, in the tenth and eleventh centuries, women—even noble women—lost status in western Europe. They were generally not allowed to control lands and property, which they had been able to do before. In the tenth and eleventh centuries, men were valued for their military skill. Women, as a result, were devalued. In addition,

Double Monasteries

In double monasteries, where monks and nuns lived in separate parts of the same complex, the work was divided between them. Nuns cared for any children or elderly people living in the monastery. They also met the needs of travelers staying as guests. Monks tended to do manual labor. One reason for the rise of these institutions was that only men could be priests and lead Mass. Thus, nuns needed to have priests nearby. Most of these institutions began as convents, with the monks added later.

▲ This symbolic painting shows the four virtues—(*from left*) Prudence, Temperance, Fortitude, and Justice—teaching nuns how to care for the ill. Caring for the ill was part of monastic life from the start. Benedict included a guest house for the care of the sick in his monastery at Monte Cassino. Most such institutions in the Middle Ages were run by monasteries.

writings by Church leaders began to describe women as the source of temptation who would lead men to sin. With women's loss of status, double monasteries became less common. They revived in the twelfth and thirteenth centuries, but were this time led by men and not by women.

Monasteries that were part of the reform movement set up separate establishments for women. A Cluniac convent was founded in 1063 in Marcigny (France). The nuns were all from the high nobility, but they followed the strict discipline and austerity that Cluny was known for in its early years. The Cistercians began establishing convents in the mid-1100s, and by the end of the thirteenth century, the order had more convents than monasteries and more nuns than monks.

THE NEGATIVE VIEW OF WOMEN

"We and our whole community of canons, recognizing that the wickedness of women is greater than all the other wickedness of the world . . . have unanimously decreed for the safety of our souls . . . that we will on no account receive any more sisters."
Conrad, abbot of Marchtal of the Premonstratensian order, late 1100s [9]

Fontevrault and Prémontré

The stories of two orders for women show the difficulties that convents faced in the twelfth and thirteenth centuries. Even when a convent grew and was successful, that very success often brought problems.

Around the year 1100, a preacher named Robert of Arbrissel founded the convent of Fontevrault in western France. It originally housed women from all walks of life, including the poor and those suffering from leprosy. Noble women gave generously to the convent, helping it to survive. Over time, their gifts led them to exert more influence on the convent and eventually to control it. Fontevrault grew in size and became physically attractive when new buildings were constructed. It also developed a less-strict way of life. The order founded related houses elsewhere in France, England, and Spain. The growth of Fontevrault was remarkable, but the order lost its original goal of providing a religious home for women from all levels of society.

the Well-Off Nuns

One of the wealthiest convents was Fontevrault, in western France. Founded on the lands of the counts of Anjou, the convent housed women from the most noble families, which gave generously to support their daughters. The counts of Anjou contributed funds as well, partly for selfish reasons—the convent held the family tomb. Late in her life, Eleanor of Aquitaine (who had been both queen of France and then later queen of England) settled at Fontevrault. She is buried there between her husband King Henry II, who was also Count of Anjou, and her son, Richard I, both of them kings of England.

The order of Prémontré is an example of how male attitudes made life difficult for women in convents. Almost from the start of the order, in around 1120, it included double monasteries. The convents became very popular. One writer from the time claimed that one thousand women belonged to the various houses. The order, however, did not provide enough money for the convents, which suffered. Within about twenty years, the head of the order shut down the double monasteries and forced the women to move to separate facilities away from the men. In the 1190s, the order decided not to accept any more women members. Those already part of the movement were not expelled, but it was clear the convents would disappear eventually. This change was the result of the negative attitude the Church had about women at the time.

The Beguines

Another movement arose in the twelfth and thirteenth centuries that tried to meet women's needs for religious life. Called the Beguines, they were not exactly nuns since they never took vows or followed any rule. Members were laywomen who gathered together to live pious lives doing good works to help the unfortunate. The Beguines differed from most nuns in two other ways. The members tended to come from the new middle class that was emerging in the merchant towns of Belgium and the Netherlands. The other difference was that the Beguines lived and worked in towns, not in the countryside.

Some Church officials praised the Beguines. They argued that these women practiced holy lives that should be models for all women. Others were not so sure. The sight of women helping meet the spiritual needs of people bothered other Church officers. Bishop Bruno of Olmütz, Germany, said, "I would have them either married or thrust into an approved order." Some councils of bishops even moved to try to ban the groups. In the end, the Beguines were accepted, but they had to agree to put themselves under the supervision of the clergy. Many houses of Beguines joined with two new male orders that were arising in the cities—the Franciscans and the Dominicans.

▶ The church at the abbey of Fontevrault shows how handsome this abbey full of noblewomen became. When founded, Fontevrault was a double monastery ruled by an abbess. The monks and priests in the male part of the institution were provided by the founder to serve Mass to the nuns.

the Military Orders

I n 1095, Pope Urban II announced the First Crusade, asking knights to fight Muslim forces in the eastern Mediterranean. The goal was to gain control of the Holy Land. For the next two centuries, several Crusades took place. In the midst of this struggle, new kinds of religious orders arose. They combined the values of knights— combat and valor—with those of monks—life according to a rule and devotion to God's work.

Holy Pilgrims

The First Crusade met some success, as the European armies captured several key spots in the Holy Land, including the city of Jerusalem. Crusader armies continued to fight to gain control of more of the countryside. In the meantime, **pilgrims** began flocking to Jerusalem and other sites sacred to Christians. Bands of Muslim fighters, however, still roamed the area,

and they sometimes attacked those pilgrims. A French knight named Hugues de Payens decided to protect the pilgrims. He gathered a group of fellow knights in 1119 or 1120. The European noble who had become king of Jerusalem allowed them to stay in some buildings on the site of the ancient Temple of Solomon, and the knights came to be called the Knights Templar.

◀ This fifteenth-century painting shows a view of Muslim armies crossing the river to attack Christian soldiers during the First Crusade. The Crusades led to the creation of new kinds of orders that combined the discipline of monastic rule with a dedication to fighting on behalf of Christianity.

The Knights Templar

In just a few years, the Knights Templar won the praise of Bernard of Clairvaux for their work. Their ranks swelled, increasing even more when they decided to organize themselves as a new kind of order—a military order. The Templars took vows of chastity, obedience, and poverty. They also took a vow to assist the helpless and to fight all enemies of the Christian Church.

The Templars developed an organization that was highly structured. They set up chapters, called temples, in every town in the Holy Land that Christians controlled. A commander led each chapter, but he owed obedience to the grand master who headed the order. In 1139, Pope Innocent II declared that the Templars owed obedience directly to him. As a result, they did

▲ Crusader armies assault Muslim defenders of Jerusalem in 1099. The Christian capture of this city and nearby sites led to an influx of pilgrims from Europe to the Holy Land. The military orders arose to care for and protect these pilgrims.

A HOLY KNIGHT

"Without doubt, fortified by both arms [weapons and faith], he fears neither demon nor man. Nor indeed is he afraid of death, he who had desired death. . . . If the cause of the fighting is good, the consequence of the fighting cannot be evil."
Bernard of Clairvaux on the Knights Templar [10]

35

not have to answer to any bishop in whose area they had lands, which allowed them to act without interference.

Growing Power

The Templars grew to be very large—up to twenty thousand knights. Gifts from nobles and kings gave them lands in many kingdoms. They became bankers and moneylenders in the Holy Land and Europe, gaining even more power and wealth.

During the 1180s, Muslim armies gained strength and started to push the Christian armies out of Jerusalem and other key spots in the Holy Land. The wars continued through the thirteenth century until, in 1291, the last Crusader stronghold fell. In the last years of the Christian state, the Knights Templar moved much of their wealth out of the Holy Land and into France.

In France, King Philip IV decided to move against the Templars, and in 1307, he arrested all its members within his lands, accusing them

of heresy and various crimes. Philip, whose treasury was low, hoped to gain the Templars' wealth for himself. Kings in England and Castile (part of modern Spain) acted in the same way. King Philip put pressure on Pope Clement V to act against the Templars as well, and in 1312, the pope abolished the order. Many knights were arrested; others joined other military orders. The pope declared that most of the Templars' fortune should be given to another military order, though Philip IV received a sizable share. The Knights Templar existed no longer.

The Hospitallers

The order that received most of the Templars' wealth was the Order of the Hospital of Saint John of Jerusalem. They are often called the Hospitallers. This group began before the Templars, though it was not a military order when first formed.

In 1070, a group of Italian merchants founded a hostel in Jerusalem to care for Christian pilgrims. When the Crusaders captured Jerusalem, the monk who then ran the hostel won for his group a grant of land and buildings in the city. Soon the group acquired lands in Europe and set up hostels there for people preparing to go on a pilgrimage. In 1113, the pope recognized the group as an order that answered only to the papacy. In the 1120s, the Hospitallers began taking on military assignments, defending

◀ Philip IV (wearing a crown and red robes on the left) watches as Jacques de Molay—once the powerful head of the wealthy Knights Templar—is burned for heresy in March 1314. The king himself died that same year.

Krak des Chevaliers

Towering on a hill in western Syria, near the border of Lebanon, is the impressive castle of the Hospitallers, Krak des Chevaliers. The name Krak des Chevaliers, which combines French and Arabic words, simply means "Castle of the Knights." The structure had originally been a Muslim fortress. It was captured by Crusaders in 1109 and given to the Hospitallers some years later. The military order enlarged it enough to be able to hold as many as two thousand fighters. They strengthened the structure, giving it two rings of thick walls, which had a moat between them. Despite these efforts, the impressive castle did fall in 1271 to Muslim fighters.

▲ The imposing castle Krak des Chevaliers was thought to be unconquerable. It was huge and built high on a hill with thick stone walls. In the late thirteenth century, however, after Jerusalem had fallen to the Muslims, the Hospitallers surrendered the castle to a Muslim army after a short siege.

Moving On

When Acre, the last city held by Christians in the Holy Land, fell in 1291, the Hospitallers fled the area. They settled on the island of Cyprus but soon after moved to Rhodes, where they remained from 1307 to 1523, taking the name the Knights of Rhodes. From that base, they sent out fleets to harass Muslim shipping in the Mediterranean. In 1522, Muslim forces laid siege to Rhodes, and on January 1, 1523, the knights left the island. They wandered for a few years until, in 1530, the Holy Roman Emperor gave them the island of Malta. Settling there and focusing on their charitable work, they became the Knights of Malta. They continue to do charity work today.

Christians from Muslim attacks and blocking raids by Muslim forces. Eventually it, like the Knights Templar, became a military order. The order also came to control many castles in the Holy Land.

the simple life

he thirteenth century saw the rise of two new important orders. Like monks, members of these orders followed rules and eventually lived in group homes, but both of these orders had different missions from those of monks. These orders—the Franciscans and Dominicans—reflected changes in European society and in the Church.

Changes in Europe

By the thirteenth century, the Roman Catholic Church had grown wealthy and powerful. Many high-ranking Church officials lived luxuriously. Popes ruled over some lands like secular lords and were deeply involved in politics. The crusading spirit had lessened. To some people, the Catholic Church had become corrupt and worldly. There was also a rise in heresy, or beliefs that differed from official Church doctrine. Some of these beliefs challenged the authority of Church officials.

At the same time, European society was changing. The eleventh and twelfth centuries saw the medieval economy grow. Agriculture still dominated the economy, but manufacturing, especially of textiles, was gaining importance. Trade between different areas of Europe increased, which helped towns grow. Townspeople had more freedom than serfs, who were bound to their lord's land. Many of those living in towns also had more education than rural people. Some of these town dwellers were unhappy about the power and wealth of the Church.

Many people still had deeply held religious beliefs, however, and were inspired by stories of the struggles of the apostles—Christ's followers who had first taught the faith. They hoped that adopting a simpler life, like the apostles' lives, would bring them closer to God. In this society, a new kind of religious order arose. Members of this new order were called friars (brothers).

The Birth of the Franciscans

The new order was launched by Francis of Assisi, and members of the order became known as Franciscans. In his twenties, Francis dedicated

Francis of Assisi
(c. 1181–1226)

The founder of the Franciscan order was the son of a wealthy merchant in the Italian town of Assisi. As a child, Francis wanted to become a knight, but in his twenties, he abandoned that plan, along with his father's dream that he would enter the family business. Feeling a deep spiritual change, Francis began giving away money and possessions and helping the sick and poor. Confronted one day by his angry father in the center of town, Francis took off his clothes and handed them to his father. He had set himself on a course of poverty. For the next several decades, Francis preached and taught a growing group of followers. He died young, his body no doubt weakened by his life of poverty and his frequent fasting.

himself to a life of poverty, preaching, and good works. He quickly gathered followers who were inspired by his sincerity and simple message. In 1209, he asked Pope Innocent III to give formal permission to the movement to continue, which the pope did.

Franciscan practice differed dramatically from that of earlier monks. Rather than vowing to remain in a monastery, Franciscans moved from place to place. Instead of growing food on monastery lands and living in monastic rooms, they begged for food and shelter each night. Monasteries had become wealthy establishments, and monks like those at Cluny were dressed in

habits of the finest cloth. Franciscans chose poverty to better imitate the purer life of the apostles. They dressed in coarse brown robes tied at the waist with a simple piece of cord and walked barefoot.

Franciscans also differed in their mission. Monks devoted their days to prayer, whereas friars spent their time preaching. Like monks, friars were driven by the desire to lead a spiritual life.

The Franciscans inspired many to join the order, but they also appealed to the broad

▲ This painting shows two images of Francis of Assisi. On the far left, Francis, pointing to heaven, preaches to a group of birds. He was famous for his gentle manner with animals. In the center, he blesses a group of people who represent the town of Montefalco (Italy), which is shown in the background.

audience who heard them preach. For centuries, the Church had viewed monks and nuns as the best example of Christian faith. It placed little spiritual value on the ordinary lives of the vast majority of people, who lived and worked in the world, married, and had children. The

THE CALL OF POVERTY

"The brothers shall appropriate nothing to themselves, neither a place nor anything; but as pilgrims and strangers in the world, in poverty and humility serving God, they shall with confidence go seeking alms."
Franciscan Rule [1]

Franciscans preached that ordinary people could adopt a simpler life and do penance for their sins while still living in the world. In this way, they could win salvation.

Franciscan teaching also led to several traditions now common to the Roman Catholic Church. Francis himself helped popularize the nativity scene, showing the baby Jesus in a manger with Joseph and Mary nearby. The **stations of the cross** that appear on the walls of Roman Catholic churches became prominent because of the Franciscans.

Growth and Change

The Franciscan movement grew rapidly in northern Italy. Within just ten years, Francis had as many as five thousand followers. Most came from the laity, not from the clergy, and most came from noble or merchant families. They moved from town to town, preaching in town squares and begging for food. At a large meeting in 1217, the friars decided to take their mission into the larger world. They divided Europe into regions and appointed leaders and assistants in each region. In 1223, the pope approved a rule for the Franciscans to follow.

As the order grew and spread, it changed. Many university students joined, and they pushed the Franciscans to place importance on teaching as well as preaching. Priests became a dominant force in the order, though lay members were still accepted. Eventually the order accepted the idea of having communal houses where friars could live permanently. By the early fourteenth century, Europe had about fourteen hundred Franciscan houses.

The Poor Clares

A woman named Clare from Assisi in Italy was inspired by the preaching of Francis to adopt his life of poverty and spirituality. She took her vows and established an order for women. The first rule for this order was based on Benedictine ideas and had been drawn up by a cardinal. It allowed the community of women to own property so they could have a place to live; the Church did not want women on the streets begging for a place to stay. Clare won approval for a stricter rule just days before she died.

About ten years later, a new rule was adopted that relaxed some of these restrictions. The order split between those who accepted Clare's Rule—called the Poor Clares—and those who followed the somewhat less-strict rule—called Urban Clares. Both groups lived in communal houses and were cloistered, meaning they had little or no contact with the outside world.

Clare of Assisi
(1194–1253)

When Clare of Assisi was eighteen, she was preparing for a marriage her parents, who were local nobles, had arranged. With no desire to carry out the wedding and inspired by Francis's teaching, she fled the family home. Reaching Francis, she convinced him to take her into the order. Many women followed, including her mother and sister. According to legend, her prayers and devotion to God twice saved Assisi when it was under attack.

▶ In this painted panel, Clare of Assisi stands in a gown far richer than anything she wore after taking her vows. She was not only a follower of Francis but also a counselor to him. Once, when he considered giving up his mission of preaching, she convinced him to continue his work.

The Dominicans

Another order of friars arose in the early thirteenth century. These were the Dominicans, named for their founder, Dominic de Guzman of Spain. Born to a noble family, Dominic became a priest and was educated in a Spanish university. He was concerned about the Cathar movement, which harshly criticized the Church for its wealth and power and urged followers to adopt the simple apostolic life. The Church said the Cathars' beliefs were heresy, or false teaching. Cathars believed the devil was as powerful as God. Church officials worried because the movement was gaining popularity, especially in southern France. Dominic reasoned that the best way to combat the heresy was for the Church to offer an example of the simple holy life as well. Preaching by such people, he thought, would be more convincing.

Dominic and his followers, who became known as the Dominicans, adopted a rule and were recognized by the pope in 1216. The following year, they decided to spread across Europe. Dominic took an important step when he sent some members to the cities of Bologna and Paris—home to two growing universities. Studying **theology** and recruiting talented students became key features of the order. The Dominicans designed their rule to fit their

◄ Dominic, on the left and pointing down to the fire, is shown directing the burning of books owned by the Cathars, the group the Church charged with heresy. The movement against the Cathars inspired Dominic to form the Dominican order.

Governing the Dominicans

The Dominicans' organization had an unusual feature, which was how leaders were chosen. Benedict's Rule had urged that all monks choose their abbot, but this principle was not always followed. Dominicans adopted the practice and carried it further. The friars in each chapter chose both the prior who headed it and his assistant. Each year, all the priors in the region attended a meeting, where they elected the regional head. Other officials higher in the order, including the master general who headed all Dominicans, were also elected. The whole structure was a remarkable example of democratic ideas.

mission of preaching and studying. For instance, they spent less time taking part in the Divine Office so they could have more time for studying. Like the Franciscan order, the Dominicans spread across Europe. Within one century of its founding, the order had about six hundred houses and perhaps twelve thousand friars.

Changing Roles

Over time, many Franciscans and Dominicans became learned in theology. Thomas Aquinas, one of the most famous teachers of the Middle Ages, was a Dominican—as were many other medieval scholars, including Albertus Magnus and Roger Bacon. Bonaventure, a Franciscan,

THE DIFFERENCE BETWEEN FAITH AND REASON

"The reason why science and faith cannot be about the same object, and in the same respect, is because the object of science is something seen, whereas the object of faith is the unseen."
Thomas Aquinas, *Summa Theologica* [12]

▲ Bonaventure was not just a respected teacher; he became head of the Franciscan order in 1257. He is shown here wearing the robes of a cardinal bishop, a very high Church office to which he was appointed in 1273.

was also highly regarded as a teacher.

In 1233, the religious learning of the Dominicans and Franciscans led them to become involved in newly formed Church courts, called the **Inquisition**. These courts wanted to find and punish those guilty of heresy. Friars who had a deep understanding of theology were ideal candidates to carry out the work of the Inquisition, because they were able to spot ideas that did not fit official Church doctrine.

The friars, then, came to play important roles in the Roman Catholic Church. They did not replace the work of monks and nuns though. Those people continued to devote themselves to lives of prayer and work, believing that by doing so they were saving other people's souls.

357-358
Basil of Caesarea visits holy communities in Egypt; his writings about them help spread the idea of a community of people following a spiritual life.

c. 410
First monastery is founded in western Europe at Lérins, France.

c. 535
Benedict of Nursia begins composing his Rule.

c. 540
Cassiodorus founds a monastery in Italy, where he instructs monks to collect and copy texts.

590-604
Gregory I serves as pope; during this time, Gregorian chant is formalized.

c. 600
Columbana writes his Rule.

674-682
Benedict Biscop founds monasteries at Wearmouth and Jarrow, England.

793
Viking attack on Lindisfarne opens period of Viking raids that weaken monastic movement.

910
William of Burgundy grants land and independence to the reform monastery at Cluny, France.

933
Reform monastery is founded at Gorze, France.

1063
First Cluniac nunnery is founded at Marcigny in France.

1084
First Carthusian monastery near Grenoble, France, is founded.

1088
Odo of Cluny becomes pope, taking the name Urban II.

1088-1130
Abbot Hugh builds a new church in Cluny, which is the largest church in the world at the time.

1095
Pope Urban II calls for the First Crusade.

1098
First Cistercian monastery is founded at Citeaux, France.

c. 1100
Robert of Arbrissel founds Fontevrault for women.

c. 1112
Hildegard of Bingen takes vows as a nun.

1113
Pope recognizes Hospitallers as an order owing obedience to papacy.

1115
Bernard leaves Citeaux to open Cistercian daughter house at Clairvaux, France.

1119-1120
The Knights Templar is founded to protect pilgrims in the Holy Land.

c. 1120
The first community of Premonstratensians is founded; houses for women are founded as well.

1120s
Hospitallers become a military order by taking on military duties.

1139
Pope Innocent II places Knights Templar directly under control of papacy.

1147
Hildegard founds a convent near Bingen in Germany.

1150
Some groups of canons regular adopt the Rule of Augustine, becoming the Augustinians.

1197-98
Premonstratensians decide that no more women should enter the order.

1209
Pope Innocent III gives permission to Franciscans to carry on their mission.

1212
Clare of Assisi takes vows as a Franciscan.

1216
Pope Honorius III recognizes the Dominican order of monks and nuns.

1223
Pope Honorius III approves the Franciscan Rule.

1233
Dominicans and Franciscans begin to take part in the Inquisition.

1307
Hospitallers establish themselves on Rhodes.

1312
Pope Clement V abolishes the Knights Templar.

1523
Knights of Rhodes (formerly Hospitallers) forced to abandon Rhodes by Muslim army.

Source References:

[1.] C. Warren Hollister, *Medieval Europe: A Short History*, Wiley, 1964, p. 1

[2.] The Benedictine Rule, quoted in J. A. Hoeppner Moran Cruz and R. Gerberding, *Medieval Worlds: An Introduction to European History, 300-1492*, Houghton Mifflin, 2004, p. 127

[3.] The Rule of Columbana, quoted in F. D. Logan, *A History of the Church in the Middle Ages*, Routledge, 2002, p. 27

[4.] Quoted in F. D. Logan, see above, p. 82

[5.] William of Burgundy, quoted in J. A. Hoeppner Moran Cruz and R. Gerberding, see above, p. 258

[6.] Bernard of Clairvaux, quoted in C. H. Lawrence, *Medieval Monasticism: Forms of Religious Life in Western Europe in the Middle Ages*, 3rd ed., Longman, 2001, p. 148

[7.] Orderic Vitalis, quoted in J. P. McKay, B. D. Hill, and J. Buckler, *A History of Western Society*, 6th ed., Houghton Mifflin, 1999, p. 322

[8.] William of St. Thierry, quoted in C. H. Lawrence, see above, p. 68

[9.] Quoted in R. W. Southern, *Western Society and the Church in the Middle Ages*, Penguin Books, 1970, p. 314

[10.] Bernard of Clairvaux, quoted in J. A. Hoeppner Moran Cruz and R. Gerberding, see above, p. 305

[11.] Fransiscan Rule, quoted in C. H. Lawrence, see above, p. 247

[12.] Thomas Aquinas, quoted in A. Fremantle, G. de Santillana, and S. Hampshire, (eds.), *The Great Ages of Western Philosophy*, Houghton Mifflin, 1962, vol. 1, p. 129

abbess   The female head of a convent

abbey   An independent monastery, headed by an abbot; contrast with *priories*

abbot   The male head of a monastery

anchoress   A woman hermit who lives in complete isolation in a cell

barbarian   An ancient Greek word used by Romans and later Europeans to describe foreigners. It suggests that foreigners are wild, brutal, and savage.

caravans   Travelers who group together to help each other, usually in a hostile region, such as a desert

cell   A small, simple room in which a single monk or nun lives

clergy   People recognized by a church as having the authority to perform religious services

Crusades   Wars fought between Christians and Muslims, pagans, or heretics

daughter houses   Monasteries or nunneries set up as offshoots of the main monastery of an order

Divine Office   A series of regular prayers chanted at set hours eight times a day by both monks and nuns

dowry   Money or land given by a girl's family when she marries or given to a convent when she enters it

excommunicated   Declared that a member of the Church has done something so wrong that he or she is officially expelled from the Church

fealty   In the feudal system, the oath that one person gives to a superior, in which the person pledges loyalty and support in return for protection

feudal system   The system in the Middle Ages in which knights and religious leaders were given property or payment from their lord, and in return they had responsibilities to the lord

gristmills   Mills for grinding grain

habits   The robes worn by monks and nuns; each order had a distinct color and design for its habit.

heresy   A belief that differs from official Church doctrine or orthodoxy

hermits   People who live away from other humans, usually in a wilderness

Holy Land   The area of the Middle East where Jesus lived and taught

Inquisition   A court used in the Catholic Church to find and punish people guilty of heresy; those found guilty of heresy were executed.

Mass   The religious rite that includes the ritual eating of bread and drinking of wine, which is part of Roman Catholic services; the two substances symbolize the body and blood of Jesus. The ritual recalls the last meal he shared with his apostles.

medieval   A word that relates to and describes the Middle Ages

missionary   A person who travels to new areas to preach his or her faith in the hope of winning converts

mystic   A person who seeks direct knowledge of God through prayer and meditation

oblates   Children placed in a monastery or convent for the purpose of having them learn and eventually take the vows of a monk or nun

ordained   Officially given authority as a member of the clergy

order   The entire body of monks who lived under a particular monastic rule, such as the Benedictines, the Cistercians, or the Carthusians

pagan   A term used by Christians to refer to the traditional beliefs of the Romans and Germanic peoples, which includes belief in multiple gods

papacy   The office of the pope and all the parts of the administration of the Roman Catholic Church that the pope controls

parliaments   Conferences to discuss public affairs or the organization of political groups to form a government

pilgrims   People who journey to a place of religious importance

priories   Monasteries led by a prior, which are satellites of a mother monastery; contrast with *abbey*

Roman Empire   The people and lands that belonged to ancient Rome, consisting of most of southern Europe and northern Africa from Britain to the Middle East

secular   Related to the world; secular power was that held by rulers and nobles.

stations of the cross   A series of images, usually hung on church walls, showing the stages of Christ's passion and death

theology   The formal study of religious beliefs and doctrine

Books:

Hinds, Kathryn. *The Church* (Life in the Middle Ages). New York: Benchmark Books, 2000.

McAleavy, Tony. *Life in a Medieval Abbey* (English Heritage). New York: Enchanted Lion Books, 2003.

Norris, Kathleen. *The Holy Twins: Benedict and Scholastica*. New York: G.P. Putnam's Sons, 2001.

Pernoud, Régine. *Women in the Days of the Cathedrals.* San Francisco: Ignatius Press, 1998.

Sherrow, Victoria. *Life in a Medieval Monastery* (Way People Live). San Diego: Lucent Books, 2000.

Zarlengo, Dianne, (ed.). *Living in the Middle Ages*. San Diego: Greenhaven Press, 2004.

Web Sites:

The Middle Ages

www.learner.org/exhibits/middleages

Created for the Annenberg Foundation and the Corporation for Public Broadcasting, this site has information on medieval religion that includes material on monks and nuns and on the Benedictine order.

The Middle Ages, Chivalry, & Knighthood

www.teacheroz.com/Middle_Ages.htm

This site gathers many links under topic headings. See "Religion" for several sites on monks, nuns, and monasteries. See "Important People" for links to material on Bede, Hildegard of Bingen, and Francis of Assisi.

NetSERF (The Internet Connection for Medieval Resources)

www.netserf.org

This web site has many links organized by topic. See the topics: "Religious Orders" (under the heading "Religion"); "Abbeys and Monasteries" (under "Architecture"); "Gregorian Chant" (under "Music"); and "Manuscript Illumination" (under "Art").

Videos/DVDs

Assisi, Home of St. Francis. Janson Video, 2002 (VHS).

Christianity: The First Thousand Years and The Second Thousand Years. A&E Entertainment, 2001 (VHS, DVD).

Gregorian Chant: The Monks and Their Music. Paraclete Television, 1994 (VHS).

Life in the Middle Ages: The Monk. Schlessinger Media, 2002 (VHS).